The Myth

The Nine

The Myth
&
The Nine

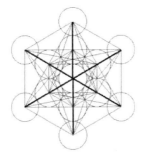

Marked these words the Quill of Hermes.

Raise the green-lipped youth, Adonis.
Listen well - as if to Eros -
See the Beauty; inner promise.

Through the self a solar system
Metes out time. The planets singing
Sealed in lines a great revision.

"LIGHT!"

The cosmic bells are ringing.

2 Green Man ceiling boss at St Helen Witton Church, Northwich, R. Lamb

Truth resounds with inner sightings
Space is scanned for skwyard giants'
Astronomic temples; Sun-signs
Trace the thread of ancient science.

There in orbit turn the star-lings -
Planets binding, suns inclining -
In such ways that whole dimensions
Fold inside the vaults of Heaven.

Angels watch the hidden star gates:
One from North, a second, South-side,
East then West. The seal is six-faced -
Secret form - A cube-shaped inside.

"Hope!"

The birds define with wisdom,
Greener words. A sidereal vision
Thus, reveals undying memories,
Log-book of a life-time's mission.

Starlight is the love inflection -
Four plus one, the whole quintessence -
Flame, Air, Water, Earth, Reflection,
Quantum leaps in five directions.

Twelve the signs that mark the time-piece,
Zodiacal months and sections.
Fiery Water, Earth-Air, Star suite.
"Now behold the Ram," says Hermes.

Vernal sun; the hide of Aries -
Golden fleece – lights Pallas, Mighty
Guardian over Argive heroes;
Asteroid of winged Niké.

This, the key to hidden gateways, –
Look beyond to see the secret -
Clio fixed, for all the greats' days
Thalia the Muse and Grace - says:

Artemis with bow and quiver
Stands aloft on Mount Olympus,
As the doe and stag, in silence,
Jump the clear and star-lit river.

Swift they run. As magic carpets
Are the green and silver forests.
Watch the bears – and bees with honey -
As the Goddess hits her target.

"Bravo, Sister!' beams Apollo -
Gazing at the sea below them -
"Never did you miss with arrow!"
'Sinks the form of bold Orion'.

Lord Apollo watches – silent -
As the virgin's beau drifts skyward.
Watches as the only question
O'er her virtue learns his lesson.

By a cedar stands she, grieving -
Bows her head in shameless weeping -
Cries upon the smelted moon beams,
Chastening her ruthless sibling.

"King of priests, my Lord Apollo,
Reasons for his death ring hollow.
While the muses – nine that love thee -
Contemplate their selves, you'd fool me!"

Laughs the god: "Your love's a martyr,"
Facing here a charging Taurus,
Tempted by the Atlas daughters,
Girls who glide on lucid waters."

Then the son of old Poseidon -
He that roused Apollo's hatred -
Shouts: "Assassin! Jealous brother,
Long it is for this you've waited.

Sun-God, you designed my downfall
Cruelly, so the breath of sorrow
Falls anew on Winter evenings,
Feeds the dew each misty morrow.

As the nymphs sang paeans, God,
You chose to then divulge my 'fortune',
Chose to fool your trusting sister,
Felled the seed of mighty Neptune.

Jealous God, you made her shoot me
while I braved the deep, the blue sea,
Just because my foot was fleeter
And my love, God, *that* much sweeter!

All shall know the truth of this:
The virgin loves, my Lord, my kiss,
The virgin loves, my Lord, my touch;
My Lord – she loves it – oh so much!"

Though her arrow caught me, truly,
She has made me quite immortal.
Greatly shall this come to haunt you;
As I stand at Heaven's portal!"

Whilst he bathes in sun, Apollo,
Concentrates Orion's sorrow,
Hail's the starry-minded brothers,
Castor, Pollux, twins of Leda.

"Fare thee well, oh son of Zeus?
And how's the child of Tyndareus?
Do me if you will, a favour,
Keep an eye on this old raver!

Hale Orion scorns the heavens,
Struggles 'gainst his fixed position.
We must give him bitter medicine,
Keep him chained in soul submission."

Starman, brave, the hale Orion,
Shouts aloud: "These boys you fancy,
Golden one, are two-faced planets!"
Now the hunter's voice is angry.

"Why, pray tell, does noble Hera
Love the clawing, crabby creature?
Why, great Zeus, defend the Lion,
That which tortured all Nemea?

Pluto, halt the poisoned creeper -
Clamp the stinging beast of Ares.
Save me from this curse, Demeter
Show me justice, I should meet her!

By Olympus, I'm surrounded -
Gods, your beasts should all be grounded!
Yet I see my dogs are pining,
Faithful hounds are there compounded."

Hearing truth, the gods, who heed it,
Forge three glyphs to raise the dog-star
High above. The bane of Thebans
Forms in flames the sign of Ishtar.

Lo, Orion, now is smiling
Down upon his faithful ally,
As the upper vaults of heaven
Blaze with light….The star's beam leavens.

"Centaur wise?" He summoned Chiron,
"Help me while away some hours,
We'll drink wine - a crimson fountain!
Then reclaim the heroes' mountain".

"Raise a cup for me." says Chiron,
"I must guard the heart of darkness.
Child of Earth in Starry Heaven
Drink of memory, shun the cypress!"

---

[3] Sidney Hall, Urania's Mirror, Canis Major & Lepus

4

From the stream that's clear as crystal,
As the knowledge dawns, he rises
From the dark, reveals his prowess,
Thinks Orion: "So, I'm timeless!

"If I'm made to stand here waiting -
Forced by ties which bind, eternal"
Hale Orion roars in fury,
"My revenge shall wax infernal!

"Long for I the Winter solstice,
When the Sea Goat meets the Sun King.
On that day the horn of plenty
Brims. How long will this event be?

"Might of oceans, old Poseidon,
Let the fishes swim beside me?
Lest you grant this one diversion,
I shall die of boredom, nightly!

"Tell me this, as well, oh wise one,
When does Hades mete out mercy -
When young Eros drinks the ocean,
Aphrodite reaches thirty,

"Hestia's hearth is icy cold,
Or Hermes sighs and says, 'I'm old;'
Hera gives her heart to Echo,
Atlas cries and lets the Earth go?"

From the swelling seas, un-silent,
Rising from the salt, through ether,
Neptune holds aloft his trident,
Sighs: "The Spring has come; be patient."

As the centre of his offspring
Glows – outraged to so be lectured –
So much wisdom of the ages
Flows from Father-Ocean's lectern:

"Take some good advice, Orion:
Watch and learn the way of heaven;
Time just moves around in circles,
From the fish becomes a turtle."

"Onward, then, we find a deluge
Caused a boar to swim the ocean.
As the lion – Narasimha -
Came before the dwarf, Vamana.

"Then to life a noble hero
Sprang, and rid the world of tyrants.
This made way for Rama, Born
In days before the Bhagavad Gita.

"In this way the prince of paupers
Broke the wheel of earthly suffering;
Maybe, son, you'll hear him teaching
In the realm of endless loving…"

Hale Orion bears this preaching -
As the son must heed his father –
Though inside, his heart's repeating:
Rules are made for fools not starmen!

Peering through the velvet darkness,
Seeks the Starman souls like-minded.
Souls who cry for freedom – partners -
Ones to rend his endless bindings.

Near yet far, he spies another
In the spiral map of Hera -
Milky star-way - whereupon is
Resting Perseus. Calls Orion:

"I have a plan to rout Olympus,
Woo the nymphs and plunder treasure,
Somehow try to storm Zakynthos,
Free the slaves and take my measure.

Maybe you – and then your brother -
Have some cause to join up forces?
Unified, we'd hold forever,
This would bring immortals chaos?"

Half a sound is made by Perseus -
Just a calm, sub-sonic murmur -
Tone of one who's done his duty:
"Starman, you are a cosmic learner.

"Peace is what we need in heaven –
This is all the wise are teaching –
Why not heed the words the water
Gave, why raise the fires against it?"

Still the Starman shuns his prison,
Rues the day his will was rendered
Helpless. Though the sun has risen,
Never shall this soul surrender!

Now Orion tries another -
One who killed the dreaded hydra -
Caught the boar of Erymanthes,
Spent a life in solid labour.

"Will you see, great Herakles
That we are stronger, still, together,
Strong enough to reach Elysium;
Gods are great, but we are better?

"Surely you, from that position -
That which marks the sun's direction -
Could devise some plan to loosen
Ties which bind us in the heaven?

"Maybe you could snare the Cygnus
Or, perchance, this wild Aquila …
Else, pick up the Lyre, and swiftly;
Time does pass, but not so quickly!

"We have strength to break Olympus -
We're the ones to end their incest -
This could be the final challenge.
Will you mark my words with interest?

There's no answer to his queries,
Dionysus' brains are weary.
Cares he not for Neptune's offspring,
Wants he just to hear the girls sing.

Watches he the virgins wander -
Through the fire-dance, travel onward,
Filled with wine and honeyed nectar -
Through the magic realms of psyche.

There the nymph, sweet Ariadne
Forces him to drown his sorrow,
Charms him nightly with her beauty;
Drinks he like there's no tomorrow.

Groans the wine God: "New man, STOP!
And hush the hound, she'll turn the hops.
Mere immortal, you will end this.
Once for all now, comprehend it:

"Here – tonight - the true initiates
Drink new wine. The growing mystery
Share I then, but none could hear me;
Thanks to *you*, the maids grew teary.

"As did Phoebus' wan Priestess,
Voice of heaven, whom truth begets.
Hold your peace now, stand in silence."
Thus does end the hunter's license'.

Now a voice so fair, ascending,
Fills the air with love unending,
Rises on the silver moonbeams
Woven from Apollo's sun streams:'

"Bold Orion, Starman leaping,
How my heart for you is beating.
I have set you there so thy fame
Lights the path of this, the sky-train!"

Next she calls with gentle words
The creatures of her wooded world,
Speaks to them with tender charm
To keep the slightest safe from harm:'

"Sweet you are as honey, bee.
Bear and Stag, come follow me.
Jump with me across the river."
Seeks she souls with bow and quiver.

'Then the Goddess steps up on it -
Disc of night, the lamp of dreamers -
As the steeds with hooves of onyx
Take to flight with sweet Selene.

Draws she near to bold Orion
Hoping, thus, to soothe his temper.
Points to one, the oldest Satyr,
He the muses loved to muster.

"Bold Orion, please concede
That Crotus here – who lived and breathed -
Stands there now with arrows poised
To guard your captivated form.

"See, as well, the scales of justice,
Those with which the Lord Anubis
Weighed the souls of those departed,
Measured who should meet Osiris.

"Know thee not the queen of starlight
Calls to time: "Stand still, be halted"
Lo, she will perform the black rite,
Bring to life the king, through deep night?"

Now Apollo speaks: "Your wisdom
Shines upon a hidden meaning;
You have placed him here with reason
On the font of deeper dreaming!

"Might he not recall the last life
When the stars by which you've bound him,
Shone upon Egyptian Pharaohs,
Helped them walk the sky-place nightly?

"Isis now returns, I sense her!
'Fore the dawn; she shines intensely".
Queen of Egypt's floodlit delta,
Sirius, the healing Empress."

Then discern the Gods, Goddesses
That the one so named, 'Orion,'
Calls to mind his ancient history,
Sees the wheels of time that move on.

''Here's the truth." He thinks in silence:
"Now I comprehend my story.
"Memories of the tears of Isis
Come, and thus reveal my glory.

''More than all the Gods of Greece
Could muster; pales the golden fleece!
And yet that rogue – the Lord of tricks -
Has caught me in a spell of Nyx.

"Something must rejoin the fragments
Here in time of Egypt's ruler.
He'll release the captured psyche…"
"Feel the Force! I AM Unifying!"

Whilst Orion scans his life-line,
Golden one, Apollo, drones on,
Urging him to love the fortune
Which has favoured him, the brave one:

"Know thyself – you're *not* alone -
For stood beside Lord Zeus's throne,
Reclines the youth whose cup is flowing
O'er the Earth, and he's not going!

"Lips more sweet than finest mead
Has the fair lad, Ganymede.
This victorious prince of Troy
Is now the God's beloved boy!

"Weep as well for fair Callisto -
See the nymph in Ursa Major -
Maid of my beloved Sister?
Zeus's lust has near-destroyed her.

"Stubborn Starman, show some pity,
Cry for nymphs and others like them,
Girls I've chased for endless ages;
Pity those who grieve for Hyas!

"Then be glad the dreaded Hyrdra
Lies beneath thy feet, not higher,
Praise the Lords you're not poor Chiron,
Poisoned centaur, *noble* Titan!

"Look around thee in the Heaven -
Canine friend and sisters, seven
Comfort thee from loneliness -
Now count the stars, for thou art blessed!"

''Vain, ye *God*!' exclaims Orion,
"I've a mind to rouse my lion,
Give the beast reincarnation
End for good this indignation!

"Power of One, upraise Osiris!
Make a crown of horns from Taurus -
Fix it on the brow of Isis -
Set on Greece the ire of Horus!"

As he has this reawakening
Lord Apollo calls Prince Hermes,
Guardian over endless journeys,
He who made the turtle-lyre sing.

Whispers he to Hermes: "*Brother*,
Tell Orion wisdom stories.
Sow in him some inner vision,
Else, I fear, he could get boring."

Smoother than a bust of marble
Is the Prince's arching eyebrow.
He, the son of Maia, whispers,
"Dear Apollo, you must stop now!

Sun-God, where's your measured reason,
Has it burned your brains to ashes?
This is sport outside the season.
See his eye, the lightening flashes!

Give him peace or fear tomorrow."
Warns wise Hermes, eyes a-blazing,
"On the Greeks shall fall a sorrow,
Should Osiris' ire be wakened.

"I must pit my wits against him,
Lest the one that's overriding
Redefines the world's whole history,
Buries all our memories deeply…."

Hermes lifts a shield that's priceless -
Bids it cast a charmed reflection -
So does spy the Lord Osiris,
Youth itself, complete perfection.

He that rescued Dionysus
From the flames which killed Semele,
He the Gods, as one, depend on,
Spoke he, thus, to shape the darkness:

"King and priest of Egypt! Ruler
Of the world, you're robed in dulia,
Might I beg thee now to listen?
Lord, let time reveal its vision".

Hypnotising as the waters
From the clear and crystal palace
Of the Fairy queen and mermaids,
Is the looking glass. The Star gazed.

5

[5] Vishnu in his incarnation as Matsya, Wellcome Images

"See yourself – the face that's handsome -
Lit by all the stars of heaven?
Take thee now, the horn of plenty,
That which you requested lately.

"Drink, my Lord, relive a journey -
Govern dreams, see truth in Karma -
Know thee well that life eternal
Is the law and that is Dharma."

Spoke he well and so the ancient
One is mindful now to listen,
As the moving words of wisdom
Sow on Earth the Kalki Vishnu.

Please continue, thought he mildly,
I should know which other Earthling
Might make use of what is given.
Use the soul quite well; be risen.

Hermes needs no more persuasion
Than mere thought from this, the Star-
King,
Thus, the great magician whispered
More of love; love everlasting.

"There's a soul which doth, your High-
ness,
Overlay the sound of silence,
One who swayed the final juries
Yet was torn apart by Furies.

"One who plucks the deepest heart-string -
Thracian bard of noble standing -
He, who can't forget his first kiss;
Let him rule the deep Eleusis?

"Mayketh he the sweetest music -
Tames the winds, makes fire of ice -
He would rule with rhyme, not reason,
Seeking, sweet, Eurydice.

"Down he went, to play for Hades -
God who had the lady hidden -
Eurydice, the lovely maiden,
She, who by the snake was bitten.

"Hearing as he strummed so gently -
Sang a Dithyramb, song of heartache -
Hades' wife wept tears for twenty,
Whilst the God himself shed plenty.

Weeping like a bride, old Hades -
He that might undo the death-spell -
Said to him: "Oh Prince of Poets,
Sweeter is your song than nectar.

"Henceforth shall our guide be Eros,
God of love, your song convinced us.
So we shall release the lady,
On but one condition, only:

"You must not set eyes upon her
'Til she's reached the land above us.
Did you, Prince, take care to listen?
Hark or fail in this, your mission.

"I repeat, oh Prince, be mindful -
Lest you're tempted first to see her,
Then to cross the Styx with Charon -
You shall lose the lovely maiden."

6

---

6 The Veiled Virgin, Giovanni Strazza

29

Now does Hermes turn. Archaic
Is his smile. Osiris sees this,
Sees within it, Thoth the Ancient
Science Master, Time Atomic.

Looks he, now – the One – at Hermes,
Thinks into his mind the verdict,
Weighs the words, the vital message.
Mount Olympus quaked to hear it.

''I shall not deny the Certain
Things. These things shall be conceded:
Such as sharing life-eternal -
This, I think, by law is needed.

"Through the gift of sacred music
Orphic guides shall rise to duty,
Fill the minds and hearts of humans
Up with love, romance and beauty.

"That's the good news – more may follow -
But for now, this pill you'll swallow:
Floods are overdue, I'm thinking;
All of Egypt's hardly drinking.

"Let there be a great disaster,
Something of a future mystery,
Just to show I'm Lord and Master,
Godly King of timeless history.

"Thinks me now, it's time to end the
Wider ocean realm. Atlantic
Trading ceases now and Cretans -
I have deemed – are sacrificial.

"All the learned priests, however,
Those who keep the sacred science,
They shall sail out, free, to Egypt,
Therein teach the code's appliance.

"See, vain Greeks, the Mother Isis -
She who yields the greatest brightness,
Dawning now above the Delta.
Heralds laud the true High Priestess!

"Look into the West, fair brothers,
See the setting sun of Horus,
Falcon Prince, his eye, the secret,
Sign of Ra, whose ever-watchful?

"Lo, behold, the East, fair sisters,
See the golden calf of Horus,
Which by noon shall wax enormous,
This, the bull to beat all others!

"That, you'll find – beloved Hermes,
He who dared through time to journey -
Should be just enough to conquer
Taurus and those other monsters."

From her garden filled with flowers
Aphrodite screams in terror.
Then, the Goddess, caught off balance,
Falls into the field of Ares!

Thus, the God of War is fuming.
Anger grows inside him, booming,
So much so that grave Athena
Has to watch him blow up Thera!

As the scenes of devastation
Reach the eye of Lord Osiris
Thinks he: "I shall end a nation,
Then uphold another's rising.

"Cultured isle, the great Minoa -
Massive once but soon a shadow -
Shall become as mist to Egypt,
All forgotten but the sorrow."

All Olympus stands in silence -
Knowing that the day is over -
Watching as the face of darkness
Brings a wave from Cretan waters.

Then there is a moment's mourning -
Plus a second more for staring -
Tears are shed but others, yawning,
Tell the world they're done with caring.

Lord Apollo grasps Athena,
Whispering: "He's a fool this fellow;
Since he's freed the Greeks of Cretans
So shall rise beloved Athens!

"Praise the day we let the 'Gyptian
Take free reign of this, the Cosmos."
Then the Sun-God, Fair Apollo,
Overheard the thoughts which followed:

''I could devastate Olympus,
Cause beneath a mighty tremor,
Make the things of Earth grow frantic,
Stir up all the great Atlantic.

Thus, the lovely Aphrodite,
I should banish her to Venus.
Then, for Ares – God, explosive -
Mars is just the place to bind him.

Hera fits the great, bright walkway,
Hades, we'll consign to Pluto.
Yet the father, Old Poseidon,
Let him run his steeds on Neptune.

"Then the maidens – those with honour -
Artemis in love, Selene,
Keep thee near the world as Moon Queen,
Govern tides and turn. Athena:

You shall take the name, Minerva,
Teach the legions with your learning;
Help the Romans conquer Hellas,
Thereby, still be known as Pallas.

"Hestia, keep your honoured status,
May the Earth exalt your greatness.
You, Demeter, shall be Ceres
Govern over every season.

"Zeus who radiates with lightening,
Thunderbolts so freely striking,
Then be Jove with circles binding –
Halos – rings of dust surrounding.

"Though I shan't recall the priestess,
She who kept the holy mystery,
Shroud the oracle of Delphi
With the endless veil of history.

7

"Thus, I come to vain Apollo -
He who thinks himself the greatest -
Source of all my kindred's troubles:
Every evening bow to Isis.

From the rest you are put asunder,
'Cept for Hermes – he must wander
Close – and yet the comely Venus,
She will burn each night for heathens.

"Mars will threaten peace with war cries -
Or just gasp with thirst – in near skies,
Holding over Earth forever
Fears of war and stormy weather.

"Now, fair God, more bitter medicine:
Worshipped, though, the Sun is truly,
None shall gaze upon you or shall
See inside your mind. "Yet, moon beams,

"Shall take shape within the psyche.
Shield of Earth, your sister's mirror
Hypnotises every Earthling,
So, the secret love I'll give her.

"Henceforth, god, be void of reason -
Let your self be burning passion -
Tempered, just, in winter seasons.
All you long for turns to ashes.

"Filled with fire that's all-consuming
You shall draw the Earth unto thee,
Just because your will is stronger
Than your mind, which is no longer."

So the great unchained Osiris
Sends Apollo out of Nothing,
Up to where is Ra residing.
Rolling wheel of fate deciding.

Sevens swans with sorrow singing,
Break Apollo's heart, like Daphne.
Eros laughs: "The sun is kindling Hope
And he shall warm the Earthlings!"

In the sun occurs a fission,
Gold - Apollo's heart - is splintered,
So his endless shards of vision
Fall on Earth with light's precision.

Raise the sparks, the golden letters
Formed into a code. The hidden
Aleph first, then Beth unfettered,
Shin, the flame, with Mem and Daleth.

Yod He Vau - He now is coming –
Tet, Resh, Gimel, Chet, Nun, Tzaddik,
Lamed, Ayin, Samech, Zayin
Qoph, Peh, Kaph and Tau in Heaven.

Three within – the crown, creator -
Twelve then fixed upon the Seven.
Twenty-two from mother, nature;
Ten in mind, not nine/eleven.

Hermes watches, like a hermit
Shrouded by the cap of Hades,
Lest should be revoked his permit.
"Time repeals", he vows, She heard it.

''Brother, Lord, I only love thee,"
Isis Queen declares uprightly,
"You have framed the night with pagans,
Set them in our skies, quite nicely.

"You have made such fitting fates for
These, the ones who stole our thunder,
Yet I heard the one forgotten part;
The silver-quickening wonder!

"Lord of charm, the cunning Hermes
Touched your pride and so discreetly:
Whilst the sun of life is fettered
All his children grow up freely.

"Thus, Apollo's light shall profit
Those who measure seasons, cycles.
I, alone, shall not reposit
Secret signs for souls' revival".

Then her other half and brother
Smiles and kneels: "Beloved Isis!
Sister, bride - my only lover -
Let this not be made a crisis.

"Let the depths of Dionysus
Hidden stay; and so his mystery
Signifies our love eternal,
So he shall preserve our History.

"All who preach the resurrection,
All who speak of life, eternal,
All who walk in love's reflection,
They shall keep the faith, diurnal.

"Orpheus shall keep with thee
A vision of the deepest mystery.
As we'll share the vine shall Bacchus
Pass the knowledge down through history."

Looking through the space for Hermes,
Author of a timeless vision,
King of Egypt clicks his fingers,
Summons thus a great revision:'

''Thoth the Ancient – Time Atomic –
Cast aside the garb of Hades.
You have made a greater promise;
Once upon a time, you made it.

"Show me now the emerald shining
Deep within your mind – your greatness -
Show my wife the sacred Ibis,
Let it be: Unite the sacred."

Hermes gives himself a second
And a third, so time is taken -
Rather than make haste, unreckoned -
Pauses while the epochs waken.

When his memory serves him rightly,
Thoth the ancient speaks: "Osiris!
Fare thee well? The bits and pieces
Are as one; She loves thee. "Isis!

"How might I now be of service?"
Asks the one with dispensation.
"I should write it as I heard it,
Save in time the Nuit sensation?"

Lord Osiris, King of Egypt,
Blows a kiss and bows to Isis.
"See, my love, he'll keep the remit,
Make our endless story timeless!

Thoth, now, phrase the hidden secrets –
Thoth the priest, the Master builder –
Write the way." The sun-mind keeper,
Brings to light the Final Teacher.

"One as three, my eye is opened;
One in mind. The light of living
Looks more lovely now, than ever.
Solomon is wise and giving.

"As we break the day with sunshine,
Let the past be past, Apollo.
Warm the seed of this: The grapevine;
Let the bread of life be swallowed.

"Come, fair queen, the virgin Isis,
Wife of mine who loves me tender,
She who made me whole, my goddess,
One who is my soul defender.

"Where the sun doth shine at midnight,
In a place of cryptic splendour,
Let the mage of mathematics
Make an early learning centre.

"In my belt are three magicians
Come to praise a child, the new king,
In whose arms the vernal lamb lies.
Spring has come; the falcon Prince flies.

"Royal Stars – Antares, West light;
Formalhaut of Northern waters;
Aldebaran, Bull's Eye, East Side;
Regulus, the Solstice, South sight -

"Cross in space, the throne upholding.
Fix for Earth the four directions.
Keep in place the sign, the sun's King.
All uphold the Resurrection.

"Let the rainbow – seven colours -
Born of light, be veils for Isis.
Maiden bright, a Holy Mother;
Star more bright than any other.

"Let the veils be drawn now, Hermes,
Cloak the truth, you might encrypt it.
Keep the signs but aide the journey
Of the searching soul, the mystic.

"Draw thyself in hieroglyphics -
Found in space, the deep harmonic –
Bind in books our thoughts: Ellipses -
Angles, curves - through time atomic.

"Water bearer, step up lightly:
By your side an angel rises;
Prince of 'Peace. The star burns brightly;
One for all the King strides nightly.

"Then, at last, shall seals be broken,
Holy words shall be respoken,
Love, in Spirit, shall be woken,
Doors once closed shall thus reopen.

"No more bound the heart. Prometheus!
Free at last, the fire bringer.
As Pandora stands divested
Of all things but Hope, which lingers.

"So, Apollo's wolf shall wander
Through the forests, under cover
Of the moon. Her golden brother
Thus returns, reveals The Lover.

"Forwards backwards, time is taking
Cosmic steps through every section.
Herein find the secret waiting:
Future from the past; reflection."

Then Osiris, fully risen,
Calls to life, renews gestation,
Metes out Time with fate's precision,
Orders: "Scribe, define creation!"

Gathered round a blazing campfire -
Flame of white, like pure magnesium -
Sat a group of men of learning;
All had found their way with reasoning.

Each had spent a life in study,
Each had found his deeper wisdom,
Yet knew naught of any other's.
Each had made a spirit-prison.

Said the one who carried with him
Nothing 'cept the staff he walked with,
On his belt a carved mandala,
Set in which were grains of barley:

"Once upon a time in Asia
Did the son of Suddhodana
Leave the wheel of incarnations,
Teach the eightfold path with patience."

Answered one who bore a tablet
Made of stone. This etched upon it
Bore the ancient Faravahar -
Winged disc – and hieroglyphics:

"Once upon a time in Persia
Lived a man named Zarathustra,
True of mind and true in speaking,
Undiluted star-light seeking."

Speaking next, a bearded poet,
Stroked his chin and touched the symbols
Woven on his woolen long-coat:
Winged heart, the moon and lone star.

"Heights are reached by native mystics,
Yet the greatest peak of learning
Is our own, and few have reached it;
Sufi spinners rise by turning."

"Here upon our cloud, unknowing,"
Sighed the mystic Christian fathers,
"We watch souls from Heaven, growing,
Ever upward, past the dawn-star.

"Darkest night will never capture
Those who walk beneath the lantern
That was set by Christ. In raptures
Have our Saints recovered phantoms."

"Mani of the Moon, the Mirror,"
Spoke his priest. "A silver sliver
Of the lamp which lovers worship;
Shines the light on true believers."

"Brings to mind the Bodhisatva,"
Spoke the Buddhist, "of compassion."
"From the Eastern land of ancients,
Where the bowl of Earth was fashioned."

"What, pray tell, of Baha-ullah!"
Spoke at once the latest wise-one.
"He's accepted all the others
Gone before; the way is union?"

"This, you see", revealed the Rabbi,
"Charts a line which roughly follows
Down through time, a line of prophets,
Give or take a right-tongued Sophist.

"Eastern influences flourished
In our land, but naught surpasses
Now – or ever – true Kabbalah,
Eastern scripts were ne'er so magic!

"Not so!" claimed the Vedic master.
"Ours, the early bird of progress
`May pass through the stages faster,
Incarnating ever after.

"Vishnu, here, the force outstanding,
Krishna, there, the force transcending,
Both appear within our scripture,
Bhagvad-Gita; song unending."

"What of us," cried out the pagan,
"Surely we're the lords of mystery?
Since the early days of Egypt,
We've survived the Western history!"

"Those who claim that resurrection
Is the sole preserve of prophets,
Born beyond the ancient's timeline,
Listen well, and don't forget it:

"Old Osiris: dead then risen;
Great Demeter's daughter: risen;
Dionysus next was risen,
Then the Orphic bard was risen!"

Thus, the voices reached a clamour –
Each had made his case with vigour -
Each revealed his spirit's armour,
Each declared his god(s) the bigger.

So the Shaman stepped amongst them:
"Let us settle this forever,
Lest in man is made a schism,
Rent in woman, child and creature."

On his drum he rolled a rhythm,
Challenged all to meet his maker,
Clear of conscience visit heaven
Then return, not less, nor greater.

As the beat rolled on, relentless,
Nine – the listeners – reached inside them,
Sought to find their soul-connection,
Straight unto the gate of Heaven.

First to fly, the Sufi mystic –
With his coat of many colours –
Made a spiral of his spirit,
Through his dance amazed the others.

Where he went was felt a secret.
"Who'll rise next?" the Shaman wondered.
So the Rabbi brought his deepest
Spark to life and upward wandered.

Then the pagan pressed to vino
Bowls of grapes and drank the contents,
Chewed the leaves which brought the
dream world,
Through the skies his wakened soul
sent.

Next up went the Persian preacher -
He who knew the truth was deeper
Than the other side of reason -
Flew he swift to find his teacher.

On his cloud the grail man pondered
Long his wish to not be tempted,
Then, at last, was just persuaded;
As he left, the clouds were emptied.

The Myth & The Nine

With a palm pressed firmly downward
Both his legs a-crossed at centre,
Did the prince – a pauper – summon
Earth to witness; heaven entered.

Laughing with delight the Veda
Sang into the air a summons,
Brought a vehicle named Vimana,
Flew at once upon the sunbeams.

By the ray which crossed the cosmos,
Did the moon and he who loved it
Find in space the Truth Dimension,
Past the dipper, starry seven.

Seeing how the rest succeeded,
So the ninth himself was certain,
That he'd reach his destination
Up beyond the sky-drawn curtain.

On the Earth the Shaman shifted
Shape and let his song be silence.
Thus, was set a leopard's spirit,
Loose amongst the emerald forest.

Just beneath his leafy carpet
Slipped a serpent, shedding softly,
All its skin. This eerie presence
Passed them by, the nine in heaven.

The Myth & The Nine

Knew the souls of all the sages -
Those who heard within the silence
Purest notes of timeless music -
Golden was the sound of silence.

Soon the leopard reached the edges,
crossed the green, deep emerald forest,
Looked up at the sky of sapphire
Saw the eagle, called in spirit.

So the bird did swoop upon it,
Took the soul within the leopard,
Lifted it beyond the forest,
Past the clouds, ascending skyward.

From the greatest height a creature
Of the world might reach, the eagle
Spied a movement on the carpet
Over Earth and dived to reach it.

Deep within the endless ocean
Swam the dolphin, swift in motion,
With a haunting cry, the seeking
Spirit felt its wisdom speaking.

Hosts of angels sang a promise
'Here's eternal bliss in heaven'.
More than all they dared to dream of
Heard the sages all around them.

Music of the highest order,
Tones of never-ending beauty,
Filled the dolphin's soul completely
So it rose back into ether.

Now the circling bird, so patient,
Dived again to catch the spirit
As it reached for air, transpiring
At the dolphin's exhalation.

All at once the ones in heaven
Heard an instrument of glory,
Sounding far beyond their memories
Rolling out the timeless story.

Not a thing would they remember
Of the secrets of the music
'Cept that it was more than wisdom,
More than knowledge; all that truth is.

As their consciousness grew thinner,
So the eagle scanned the mountains,
'Til it spied a pair of antlers,
Saw the stag to bear the spirit.

Folded wings became an arrow
Tipped with plumes of golden feathers.
Startled though the stag was, doubtless
Was the soul which leapt upon it.

The Myth & The Nine

By the silver moon of Mani
Did the stag with spirit wander
'Cross the deep green emerald forest,
There to find the Shaman's body.

By the campfire, dying embers
Glowed just like the sun does setting,
Wakened by a moth, the Shaman
Tapped his drum to reach the sages.

Piled he high upon the fire
Dried up leaves and tinder-branches,
Blew upon the peaceful faces
Of the sages smoke, whilst dancing.

Lifeless seemed the ones before him -
Saw the Shaman, deeply breathing,
But were bathed in light of silver -
All around them stars were gleaming.

"What's the use?" spoke out the Shaman,
"Each set out to meet his maker,
Now on Earth are white-washed spirits,
Blown out minds, who seem as strangers.

"And, I see, the thrall of blissful
States is tempting. Two remain there,
Lying still in deep hypnosis,
Thinking not; they're quite unconscious!"

Chanted, then, the single Shaman
Words, recalled his greatest magic:
Brought from yonder plane of dreaming
Sages seven from the heaven.

"Make a circle, watch the fire,
Round it form a chain together,
Listen – hear – the holy drum speaks;
Rhythm forms, the sacred heart beats."

Thus, they made a single circle
Round the pile of glowing embers,
Let the drums recall the rhythm
Of the heart that time remembered.

"We're as one." They spoke in chorus,
"Though the paths we followed differed,
There was but one destination,
Now, united are the nations."

As the Shaman tapped the deer-skin
Drum, he spoke aloud his thinking,
"What became of those two fellows,
Those who still remain in heaven?"

From the green deep emerald forest,
Stepping softly came a figure,
Made of light, a horseback rider,
In one hand he bore an object.

"One returns," spoke out the Shaman,
"He could tell a pretty story,
Judging by the hand that's holding
Stuff of splendour, history's glory."

Robed in silence, seven sages
Watched the horseman drawing nearer,
Saw the object, clear as crystal,
Then exhaled the breath of ages.

"So are eight, but who has knowledge
Whereof number nine is waiting?"
Spoke the Shaman, at which moment
Something stirred within the forest.

Light of limb and swathed in mystery,
Dazzling in the emerald darkness,
Stepping soft upon the carpet
Came the ninth and moved among them.

Sat she down beside the fire,
Peaceful as the moon at midnight
As the eight in spellbound wonder,
Took her as their inspiration.

Eyes that once were blind in wisdom
Opened then to something greater.
How it happened, none could fathom;
How the ninth became this lady.

So, there is the greatest mystery:
Free of time and made immortal,
Born to hold the key of history;
She, who dared step through the portal.

8

[8] Connla and the Fairy Maiden, Project Gutenberg

Made in United States
North Haven, CT
13 February 2023

32528807R00036